THE WORLD'S TWO SMALLEST HUMANS

by the same author

THE SHUTTERED EYE
IN DEFENCE OF ADULTERY

JULIA COPUS

The World's Two Smallest Humans

First published in 2012
by Faber and Faber Ltd
Bloomsbury House
77–79 Great Russell Street
London WC1B 3DA

Typeset by CB editions, London
Printed in England by TJ International Ltd, Padstow, Cornwall

A CIP record for this book
is available from the British Library

ISBN 978–0–571–28457–3

2 4 6 8 10 9 7 5 3

for Andrew

What is to be done with the lost . . . but write them into being?

– Hilary Mantel

Acknowledgements

Some of the poems in this book originally appeared in the following publications: *Magma*, *Matter*, *New Statesman*, *Poetry London*, *Poetry Review*, *The Spectator*, *Being Human* (Bloodaxe, 2011), *Identity Parade* (Bloodaxe, 2010) and the *Forward Book of Poetry* (Forward, 2010). A selection of these poems has also been recorded on CD for the Poetry Archive.

I am deeply indebted to the Royal Literary Fund for their generous and timely financial support; also to Arts Council England, the Society of Authors for an Authors' Foundation award, and the directors of the Tyrone Guthrie Centre at Annaghmakerrig for a writer's residency.

'Stars Moving Westwards in a Winter Garden' was commissioned for *Dark Matter: Poems of Space*, ed. Maurice Riordan and Jocelyn Bell Burnell (Calouste Gulbenkian Foundation, 2008); 'An Easy Passage' won the Michael Donaghy Forward Prize for Best Single Poem in 2010, and a radio version of the sequence 'Ghost', broadcast on BBC Radio 3 in December 2011, was shortlisted for the Ted Hughes Award for New Work in Poetry.

My thanks, too, to Andrew Stevenson, Maurice Riordan and the wonderful Helyar group.

Contents

DURABLE FEATURES

This Is the Poem in which I Have Not Left You

This is the poem in which I have not left you.
The doors of the Green Dragon are not bolted
behind our backs; the pink-faced landlady
(may she be blessed) has not abandoned us
to the unseasonable cold, that March
evening of your thirty-seventh year.
In the gloom that hangs over South Street, in the quiet
made of the humming of streetlights and the moon,
the horn from a distant freight train does not sound;
I do not turn – my tongue is tied, my hands –
whatever there is to say is left unsaid.
And since I dare not speak, nothing transpires:
the street, in the moments after, does not shrink
to the slam of a door, the flare of an engine, you
suddenly elsewhere, you imagined, gone,
but seen, still seen (the night stretching between us),
cursing the fog on the Blackdowns, curving, finally,
into the narrow driveway of the cottage.

Our cottage, I meant to say, with its yellow walls,
its broken gate – I might have forgotten those,
and the fields and the light, were it not for the fact
that this is the poem in which we do not part,
but lie like lovers, one of whom is sleeping,
my head, as always, nearest the leaky window
through which the old sounds reach me – rain in the trees,
a gust of wind, a tipper truck, a siren
threading its way through the dark (but you'll not wake;
your ears are shut, you won't admit a thing).
Then further off, after the rain is done,
the voice of the redstart calling *do it, do it!*,
calling from the smallest tree in the garden.

The Constant Landlady

Secrets? Oh plenty – well, it stands to reason,
the place no bigger than your own front room
and the talk as goes on at the corner table,
peri meri dixi – so on and so on,
in the red plush seating, under the ever
wakeful eyes of the old 'Cue Masters'
(Roberts . . . Senior . . . Bennett . . . Mitchell . . .).
There's heads will roll and hearts will break
but I shan't say whose for I won't go squealing.

Four or five times of an evening I circle
from table to table, stacking the empties.
I'm minding my own but there'll always be somebody,
peri meri dixi, baring his soul,
sounding off over the hiss of the gas fire –
things going on as'd make your hair curl
but I never shall tell. You can say what you like –
when the lights are low and the moon-eyed sweethearts
lean in close, the plotters, the dreamers,
and the dark swims up at the little bay window
and pines to come in and the whole caboodle
glows in the street like a ship in harbour,
you can keep your Savoy, your Ritz, your Mayfair:
night after night I'm the one they return to,
so this one's for the road and whatever it leads to.
Petrum partrum paradisi tempori,
peri meri dixi domine.

Stars Moving Westwards in a Winter Garden

Your birthday comes, then hers, leaves fall,
and drift against the freezing feet
of benches at the roadside, melt,

in all the colours of burnt wood,
into the edges of verges, lanes,
retreating underground, then re-

appear, supple as tongues,
awag among the branches, and the trees
are cock-a-hoop again. You can't

keep up; you're sick with it;
the Earth lies at a tilt,
and as it orbits tips its infinite

faces to the sun. By which
skewed means the seasons come,
the seasons go. You change

your hair, your wardrobe, friends, and take
to driving home the scenic route, the window
down. You take up smoking for a second time.

One night, a holy dark
December night of frost,
you stand in the garden, sleeplessness

hovering inside you like a planet.
Somewhere in your dark-adapted mind
you hear her calling to you

quietly, as if from an upstairs window.
You push your hands down, hard into their pockets,
lift your face to the heavens' stutters and glints.

Above you, the yellow lustre of Capella;
to your left, the twins, their close, in-leaning heads,
the giant, unseen shoulder of Orion.

You have heard it said
that when we look out into space
we're looking back in time.

Whose time? Our own?
Right now you want this to mean
that the past itself is a kind of canopy

spread out on every side, in bluish black,
that somewhere in the night sky is contained,
among the million happenings

that led you here, that sudden summer storm
you sheltered from together, her small hand
too warm, too quick in yours (and yet

not nearly quick enough) beneath the oak
beside your uncle's house. How unforeseeable
those early intimacies were! And again how soon

unalterable. Or so they seemed.
So seems your present grief,
but grief also will pass – ripen and wither,

tied, as it is, like a moon, to this steady
turning of the earth through space,
away from the sun and back again, laden

with mountains, oceans, vineyards, quaysides, gardens,
and, tonight, this one particular garden
where a man stands, breathing into the shape of his loss,

though in truth he could stand for any one of us:
earthbound, heart-sore, his boots in the frost-stiffened grass,
travelling eastwards, against a background of stars.

Wardes

It's hard to imagine a house less aptly named.
Three years we lived immured by its faulty electrics,
caretakers of its two dark corridors,
the draughty rooms that opened from them, the rats
that huddled for warmth in the corner cupboards.

By daylight, peacocks strutted over the lawns.
Blown scraps of their voices reached to where my boy
double-dug rows of weed-choked flowerbeds,
and to where I stood at an upstairs casement, watching
his boot on the blade, his hands on the spade handle, working
into and into the soil. I had thought it a miracle
that anything might grow there, but it did.

Those wind-blown cries that made my blood
stop short were simple courting calls. They held
no message for us but my heart
felt the weight of them. At night the peacocks perched,
grotesquely large, in trees outside the windows.

It'll be fine again tomorrow, my sweetheart whispers
into the dark, some fifteen years ago.
It is early autumn and we two are lying
flat on the moon-drenched lawn, our eyes
fixed heavenwards; the slowly crumbling house
although we cannot see it is afloat
somewhere beneath our feet – this woman,
who is me, and her dark-haired boy.
Something about the way the light has fallen
or the way their outstretched hands seem fastened
each to each like two cut-paper dolls
tells me it's already too late to warn them,
the long day done and even the peacocks silent.

Amherst Interior

Outside her window, America burgeons –
its ports and cities and highways,
its snaking railroads. Outside,
the purple foothills of Montana

darken with log cabins and men
whose hands grow numb and redden in the water
for a flake or chip of gold as it skitters down
out of the cedar-covered mountains;

and by and by the uncountable weeds spring up
across abandoned cotton fields,
the plant heads cracking open till a jubilant
damp slides clean inside and rots the bolls.

In a shut room, with no seasons or weather, words
collect on the page like rain from the brimming
sponge of a cloud: *blot*, *dusk*, *speck*,
god, *blood* . . . Week after week

volcanoes, earthquakes, bombs
brood at the heart of the poems. The sun slips down
stage left behind the hill, the same sun hangs
over the white steeple, as surely as her nerves,

like hairline cracks, open with each tremor
now and again now while outside,
outside the dead and wounded will not stop appearing:
in corners of woods, in every weather – wind-

burned, rain-soaked, body after body
piling up against the fragile
breastworks of trenches
as if the earth has wept them into being.

Miss Jenkins

More and more, lately, when absence thickened the air
at the schoolgates, in the street, first thing on waking,
she'd think of her former calling, the way it had defined her.
In the dim, sugar-paper blur of the light,
while boiling the kettle or kneeling over weeds,
many times at dusk now (the streetlights coming on)
she'd feel herself alive, transported
once again to the bright, tall-windowed classroom,
chalky-fingered, cherished by her peers, and walking –
that brisk and rhythmic pace she adopted, all her working days.
Even in sleep, her breath would rise and fall with
the sharp pat pat of the children's feet approaching and
she'd sense – in her blood – like a counterpoint beneath it,
the slap of books upon each child-size table
whenever she set up class for their arrival.

Whenever she set up class for their arrival
– the slap of books upon each child-size table –
she'd sense in her blood, like a counterpoint beneath it,
the sharp pat pat of the children's feet approaching and
even in sleep her breath would rise and fall with
that brisk and rhythmic pace she adopted, all her working days.
Chalky-fingered, cherished by her peers, and walking
once again to the bright, tall-windowed classroom,
she'd feel herself alive; transported.
Many times at dusk now (the streetlights coming on),
while boiling the kettle or kneeling over weeds,
in the dim, sugar-paper blur of the light,
she'd think of her former calling, the way it had defined her,
at the schoolgates, in the street, first thing on waking –
more and more, lately, when absence thickened the air.

Heronkind

Whatever is desired
is grown toward:
a glimmer of fish
at the margins of rivers
and streams, or in marshes
triggers a longing –
a muted, persistent
itch in the newborn
heron which
she feels at the base of her
fledgling bill, a sense that will
persist until the optimal
fish-spearing length is reached.
From this point to
eternity her dreams
are crammed with fish
or the nervy, darting
shadows of fish.
How much less complex
life would be
without this feverish
dance between
the wanter and the wanted,
though the truth of it is
that without fish
all heronkind would
be stunted.

Impossible As It Seems

Once again, in the heart of the crumbling
Ile de la Cité,
in the spot where Héloïse and Abelard
began, oh dear, began to fall in love,
a simple song is drifting
into a tree-lined quai:
tum túm ta-ti túm;
the wind conveys it
through numerous breeze-blown shadows
the length of the lane:
O *amour, mon amour,* from the half-open
door of the Café of Madame Duchesnois
whose ordered rows of chocolate désserts
gleam from the window at passers-by.

And on benches in Obiralovka,
as happens each summer,
skirt-hems are rustling
over the legs of young women
not more than a two-minute walk away from the station
where Anna Karenina crossed herself slowly and
sank to her own pretty knees
in the name of lost love, in the path
of an oncoming train.

Likewise, on a certain sunlit square in Verona,
bells chime, money changes hands,
and outside the pink-hued church, a queue is forming
for a man with a pushcart frying up slices of pizza.
An inch to the right of his heel,
a message in English
is chalked at a slant on the pavement –

This is the place
where Juliet walked
out of the daylight for good
– but is largely unnoticed, blurred
by the traffic of feet,
and at sundown this evening
the water-green fountains and lights will
come on in the usual way; why would they not?

I cannot think it is the same
in South Street.

There it is midnight still,
fog-hushed and aswim
in the gloom that hung
on every slope and ledge
the hour we parted –
the road and the stoop-necked streetlights,
the bank of cars shored up against the pub,
the stock of steadily dating reads-of-the-month
propped like miniature tombs in the blacked-out bookshop,
and the single willow tree beside the school,
its many hundred leaves curled
tight as clock-springs, littering the ground
(because how could the sun come up on such a street?).

Somewhere in that muffled dark the birds,
beneath the eaves, beneath one stretched-out wing,
would sleep, in mute unease, I thought, for good.
I thought the schoolchildren would take to their beds
with a sudden, incurable illness.
Of course, they did not.
Impossible as it seems, world does not pause
to grieve for us: the minute you turned,
were gone, cool air rushed in,

black shadows reconvened
across the space where you had been.
And, now that I trouble to notice,
world is teeming
with similar gaps, backdrops
for lovers parting –
this lamplit avenue, that riverpath . . .

Today, on the site of Dido's funeral pyre,
a man at a kiosk buys the local paper,
the crackling sound it makes in this dry heat
echoing roundly off the surrounding buildings –
a perfect rhyme. He rolls it under his arm
and starts for home, his two feet urging him onwards.
But because his heart grows
suddenly cold from time to time –
and does so now – a stone, clenched
in the fist of his chest,
he pauses, bends to light a cigarette.
Somewhere in his mind a song
is starting – much too faint and afar,
at first, to hear, but as he straightens
(a thread of blue smoke rising
into the air)
he catches it once more
and, straining, leans
a little closer in –
the tilt of the light,
a soft wind through the trees –
begin again, it says; and again: *begin*.

Now Winter Is in Me

Now winter is in me, I make a pact with life,
its whimsical habits, its rhythms of freeze and melt.
I surrender again to the old and buried loves

(without whom I am nothing) now January gales
strip the drowsing snow from each branch. Snow falls
in clumps from the gleaming bonnets of cars

edging into the stream of traffic and blows
from roofs and makes the blue slate shine.
My branches coruscate with each new blast.

An Easy Passage

Once she is halfway up there, crouched in her bikini
on the porch roof of her family's house, trembling,
she knows that the one thing she must not do is to think
of the narrow windowsill, the sharp
drop of the stairwell; she must keep her mind
on the friend with whom she is half in love
and who is waiting for her on the blond
gravel somewhere beneath her, keep her mind
on her and on the fact of the open window,
the flimsy, hole-punched, aluminium lever
towards which in a moment she will reach
with the length of her whole body, leaning in
to the warm flank of the house. But first she
steadies herself, still crouching, the grains of the asphalt
hot beneath her toes and fingertips,
a square of petrified beach. Her tiny breasts
rest lightly on her thighs. – What can she know
of the way the world admits us less and less
the more we grow? For now both girls seem
lit, as if from within, their hair and the gold stud
earrings in the first one's ears; for now the house exists
only for them, set back as it is from the long, grey
eye of the street, and far away from the mother
who does not trust her daughter with a key,
the workers about their business in the drab
electroplating factory over the road,
far too, most far, from the flush-faced secretary
who, with her head full of the evening class
she plans to take, or the trip of a lifetime, looks up now
from the stirring omens of the astrology column
at a girl – thirteen if she's a day – standing

in next to nothing in the driveway opposite,
one hand flat against her stomach, one
shielding her eyes to gaze up at a pale calf,
a silver anklet and the five neat *shimmering-*
oyster-painted toenails of an outstretched foot
which catch the sunlight briefly like the
flash of armaments before
dropping gracefully into the shade of the house.

This Silence Between Us

This silence that lies between us like a body
that long ago gave up responding to pain,
still less to light (which is pain's opposite),
that cannot hear and cannot be awakened,
that is, in fact, incontinent and catatonic,
but nonetheless demands to be sat beside
and talked to, prayed for, cried over, whose limbs
and torso must be gently sponged, forehead
smoothed, even in the dead of night –
especially in the dead of night – this silence,
how long do you suppose it can continue?

Miracles happen. Today (and not for the first time)
I remember the story of Jan Grzebski
who woke one summer after nineteen years.
But it's his wife I picture, crossing the hallway
for nearly two decades – the slap of her feet
along the narrow passageway, the slop
of water in a plastic bowl till the morning when, half-
asleep, she recalls she's left the shutters open
and the window lifted where a thin net curtain
shivers in dusty sunlight as slowly the bedstead,
the bulk of the body, zigzag into place in the frame
of the doorway: sunlight, body, counterpane, all of it's
just as it should be but – dear God! His eyes!
Like two bright fish aswim in the propped-up head.

There are those who say that miracles are born
of faith, that trust alone might make you turn
and talk again . . .

I lie down next to my body
so close I think I smell its sour breath.
Still here, I whisper, but it does not stir.
Then gently, with a fingertip,
I lift one leathery eyelid
where the soul is crouched
and speak to it directly. – Not a flicker,
but it does not faze me.
It is only a matter of time before one of us wakes.

The Orange Rug

for Antony and David

Impossible to picture a time without it there
beneath the living room window, afloat in the shadows
of our father's desk. Its flattened tassels were the rays of sun
in a child's drawing; it was where we must gather,
three breathless children, our coats on for school,
or to show who was first to be ready for bed,
and if we'd a score to settle
this was where we must do it.

When was the last time we stood there,
myself and my two fly brothers,
in the days before their bodies hardened and wives
and children hovered round them?
It is late, perhaps – a splash of moon at the window.
Outside, a row of curtained houses
looks blindly away from two small boys and their sister,
who have not even thought to arrange the order
of their going. Nonetheless there must be one
who steps off ahead of the others, as if at some whisper
from the wings, and does not think to look back.

Tonight, in the small hours, I stand there again
in the shadows that leaked from the oak-dark desk;
only this time I am stiller, keener, I'm
poised, like Cassandra – listening out
for those wily, soft-voiced exit cues,
with both knees locked, my fists and eyes
squeezed, clenched, so that nothing exists
but brothers and me and the orange rug,
round as a spotlight, round as a sun,
and the hum of its solar wind unspent inside it.

Raymond, at 60

The 185 from Catford Bridge, the 68 from Euston –
those same buses climbing the hill long into the evening.
This is what stays with him best now, this and watching,
in the ward where Mother had finally died,
the way the rain had fallen on the window –
a soft rain sifting down like iron filings.
The whole of that evening he'd kept his eyes fixed on the rain,
out there in the O of the buses' steel-rimmed headlamps.
Now I am I, he thought, his two dark eyes ablaze – as if he'd
  found God
the very moment she'd left him. He took off his hat,
and he put his dry lips to her cheek and kissed her,
unsettled by her warmth, the scent of her skin
so unexpected he found himself suddenly
back on Bondway, crushed to her breast, in a gesture
that meant, he knew now, *You are loved.* There he was, with her
pulling his bobble-hat over his ears in that finicky way she had.
What was he? Eleven? Twelve? Too old, in any case, for her to be
holding his hand the entire short walk from the house
that first time she'd taken him down to watch the buses.

That first time she'd taken him down to watch the buses,
holding his hand the entire short walk from the house,
what was he? Eleven? Twelve? Too old, in any case, for her to be
pulling his bobble-hat over his ears in that finicky way she had
that meant (he knew now) *You are loved*. There he was with her
back on Bondway, crushed to her breast, in a gesture
so unexpected he found himself suddenly
unsettled by her warmth, the scent of her skin,
and he put his dry lips to her cheek and kissed her.
The very moment she'd left him, he took off his hat.
Now I am I, he thought, his two dark eyes ablaze – as if he'd
  found God
out there in the O of the buses' steel-rimmed headlamps.
The whole of that evening he'd kept his eyes fixed on the rain,
a soft rain sifting down like iron filings,
the way the rain had fallen on the window
in the ward where Mother had finally died.
This is what stays with him best now, this and watching
those same buses climbing the hill long into the evening:
the 185 from Catford Bridge, the 68 from Euston . . .

Memories, when Fixed

Memories, when fixed, are notoriously difficult to erase.
Indeed, they are the most durable features – other, perhaps, than
scar tissue – acquired during a person's lifetime.
– *The Oxford Companion to the Mind*

Not the lapsed summers,
the faces of childhood
sweethearts and friends,
but the difficult kind –
less supple, less
resistant altogether
to strain or the harsher
effects of the sun.
If they are recent they are
liable to redden; it isn't considered
decent to show them. And if
they are not, their skin
is so white, so
shockingly taut, we sense somehow
it isn't right, we feel we ought
to keep them
hidden. Yet every so often
we throw off caution: a cropped
sleeve reveals
the pale surface
we secretly hope
that someone will notice.
Perhaps we should try
to be more open.
Perhaps we could even
learn to love them,
for no amount of lotion,
oil or rubbing will
remove them.

A Soft-edged Reed of Light

That was the house where you asked me to remain
on the eve of my planned departure. Do you remember?
The house remembers it – the deal table
with the late September sun stretched on its back.
As long as you like, you said, and the chairs, the clock,
the diamond leaded lights in the pine-clad alcove
of that 1960s breakfast-room were our witnesses.
I had only meant to stay for a week
but you reached out a hand, the soft white cuff of your shirt
open at the wrist, and out in the yard,
the walls of the house considered themselves
in the murk of the lily-pond, and it was done.

Done. Whatever gods had bent to us then to whisper,
Here is your remedy – take it – here, your future,
either they lied or we misheard.
How changed we are now, how superior
after the end of it – the unborn children,
the mornings that came with a soft-edged reed of light
over and over, the empty rooms we woke to.
And yet if that same dark-haired boy
were to lean towards me now, with one shy hand
bathed in September sun, as if to say,
All things are possible – then why not this?
I'd take it still, praying it might be so.

Dig

On the final day we came at length to a layer
of packed earth. I made short shrift of it, in slices,
lifting it off with a leaf trowel to expose
a broad, flat stone. Whoever was doing the probing probed
at the stone's edge till the stick went in
and further in . . . Air breathed
its long breath over my neck; the shadows of clouds
had slid by this time onto the cooling sand.
I bent to it, chipping away at the stone with a chisel – *tap*
and *chip* . . . *tap*, *tap*, *chip* – ten minutes
or more the world was only a widening
hole leading into the dark – till one of us fed
a bare light-bulb into the gap, and pressing
my face to the stone (right cheekbone, nose, left
cheek then right again) I saw as they swam
from under the lip of the hole the reds and golds: fragments
of textiles, the shining, painted stucco.
And each person after me, who did the same, each
felt it the same: in turn, in the deep
cave of ourselves, as we looked we were lit,
utterly and for good, like a lover looking
into the eyes of one he will love,
whose hand, reaching perhaps to shoo away a fly,
brushes against her hand and is made precious.

THE PARTICELLA OF FRANZ XAVER SÜSSMAYR

a poem in four packets

In the summer of 1791 Süssmayr was staying in rooms in Baden where he had been sent to look after Mozart's pregnant wife, Constanze. While there he received, section by section, Mozart's shorthand notation of *The Magic Flute*. He translit-erated the notes into a *particella*, or short score, which he sent back in packets to Vienna for his employer to develop, refine and orchestrate.

First Packet

Do, by all means, stay awhile and catch your breath.
I saw you from the window, having just that moment
ventured to look up, for my work is nothing if not demanding.

There are places in the music, smudges and blurs,
where I cannot be certain of what is intended:
gaps at the end of the line where I find I am

translating direct from the silence. I prevail.
It is not without reason, after all, that the kapellmeister
(a woeful husband but a fine composer)

entrusts to me this delicate art of transforming
his scribbled cipher into a workable outline.
And to order! Well – I am not found wanting.

It is this that pulls me from my bed each morning
and sets me at my desk, with its view of the fountain,
the gnarled old linden tree, the glitter of the river in the
distance . . .

There is also, of course, the matter of Madame
for whose 'revival and repose' we were dispatched
last Sunday to this watery spot.

That is the story, though I have my doubts.
Twelve miles in the punishing heat in her condition!
What do you make of that? Precisely.

Yet I have never seen her so alive
as on those swaying miles away from the city,
Vienna receding – *poco a poco calando*:

at first the familiar racket and smells
and then the slowly flattening horizon
ebbed away behind the brow of a hill.

We slid back into our seats and fell to counting
the squares of fields that ripple in between
the mandatory landscape and here,

Madame crying out *scherzando* as she watched
farmhands at work on high-wheeled carts
springing to life in the lens of her quizzing glass.

The soul is freest when we are in transit,
is it not? But you must hurry now, Anton.
I hear the rattle of the mailcoach,

and the doleful tongue of the churchbell (hum,
prime and nominal) is striking twelve.
Till next time, then, and with God's grace.
Three kreutzer should suffice; it is not heavy.

Second Packet

Come in. Please. You will not, I think, be surprised
to learn that the work is done: you are a working man
yourself. Work calls – a tough and a wayward thing –

I might say tough as nettles. Yes? Like nettles in the heat
that strain, in ranks, eager as army men, towards
the sun, and must forever be cut down. Each morning

when the chimney-pots and streetlights have begun
to shoulder themselves steadily free of the dark
mass of the sky, when the washstand there has brought me

to its dogged view of housefronts, etc., the tree,
and beside it the fountain – a queer, quicksilver creature,
being made entirely, from moment to moment,

of the slender stems of water rising through her;
all her noblest thoughts, her tenderest expressions
lost in a constant downrush, only

inches from the tree – but have you noticed
how they never touch? Imagine!
The slide of water over the thirsty timber!

I digress. At such an hour, I sit, I lift my pen,
and set to the work my master has begun,
extracting from his notes the first violin,

the bass . . . Later an orchestra
will swell between them, sending out thick shoots
of harmony and counterpoint, whole detailed conversations.

I take no part in that. Detail is where the devil lies.
I feel – am I right? – a kinship of sorts between us,
insofar as we are chiefly occupied

in manual work. You transfer letters from this place
to that; I, music from a shorthand note.
A theme, a melody – these I convey

with a sharp quill to the page and fix them there:
aria, recitative – always
in outline, little skeletons

of sound. At first I used to lie awake
and try to conjure them whole, how they might end.
O how the delicate fibres of my ears

lifted and blew about in that obstinate silence!
Snagging now and then on scraps of music –
chords, motifs . . . One night my interest simply

bled away – an instant cold departure from the brain.
I saw the work for what it is. Mere nettles!
Anton, I have said we are the same

but on reflection it is afternoons
that set us apart. It is then my mistress bids me
offer her my arm and keep her safe

on the sloping walk to the waters. What a thrill
to hear in the distance, from the very
lip of the water itself, those little yelps

and squeals, the aftershocks of voices spreading out
into the pinewood under whose sweet-scented dark
we make our way. Steadily and slow.

I do not claim to sleep more easily now;
only that sleeplessness is not the scourge
it was. I lie quite still, my happy hands

curled on either side of me. And time
drips from each fingertip, the night
breeze trickles over my naked skin.
I contemplate a life of afternoons.

Third Packet

Dear fellow, you are drenched! Take a seat by the fire.
You'll join me in a glass of schnapps. Such rain!
Hand me your coat. There now. I almost think

we might be friends. These weekly chats of ours . . . Or if
not friendship, something very like it. *Prost!*
Now . . . tell me, have you ever paused to consider

the many unforeseen moments of juncture –
strangers united by joy or disaster, a walker
stalled, mid-path, by a rift, then joined to the land

by means of an improvised bridge, or again the
gap between two hesitating souls
broached by the thrown rope of a kiss?

It was yesterday afternoon, by the edge of the water:
she had stopped to pull the ribbons of her hat,
and in lifting the hat from her head she faltered slightly

and reached out a hand. At the same moment, her hair
swung loose across her shoulder, brushing against me –
accidentally, so it seemed, though I'm left with the question

is anything entirely accidental?
My fingers closed around her outstretched hand;
I remember its heat – also its smallness –

took me by surprise, and a coltish breeze;
the sky tilted about us, the voices of bathers,
for several moments, the sun . . . And then she spoke:

'A gentleman!' she said, and my gentleman shadow
bowed and tipped its hat, with a rakish flourish.
I, meanwhile, stared on dumbly after the shape of her

stepping away from me into the sulphurous water
and throwing her own hat, brim-side up, to the bank
while the skirts of her muslin bathing dress

lifted and billowed about her. On reaching the centre
she turned and fixed me with a level gaze –
five seconds – more perhaps – it's hard to say,

but in that interval everything I am
was seen and dignified and set alight.
And then the rain began, great indolent splashes,
and it was a curious thing, but nobody minded.

Fourth Packet

Take care, Anton! You need your wits about you
to pick your way between the trunk and the wall.
Forgive me; we are leaving. Back to Vienna.

The master snaps his fingers and we jump. Indeed,
there seems little point in your being here
when I can deliver the packet myself. Or can

a few hours really make such a difference? Tell me,
for I have been turning it over all morning,
what, in the end, is the world most altered by?

Many ordinary things may leave an impression –
a hall rings with the shimmering aftervoice
of a struck gong, or the faintest tremor is felt

in the earth or heart and leaves a fault.
And a thing once held by the eye, awake
or asleep, endures especially – her pale arms . . .

O there is much, Anton, more needful to the spirit
even than music, though he will not have it.
The soul itself, in that it is wafer-thin,

is shockable as litmus – yet agile too and slips
between the present and the past,
leaving a trail like pollen dust.

Well then, if we're leaving today we do not leave
entirely, for the reach of her hand and the look
that bound us briefly – all such things remain,

and the walk and the woods and the bank by the spring,
her muslin bathing skirts blooming about her
like the mind's florescence, the foam of a dream,
her upturned bonnet, filling with Baden rain.

HERO

magnus ubi est spretis ille natator aquis?
Where is that proud swimmer who spurned the waves?
– Ovid, *Heroides* XIX, 90

Now time grows long   as wool is drawn
through oily fingers   into yarn.
Or it coheres, ag-   glutinates.
Time transmutes: the waiter waits.

Dusk

I'll tell you how it is. Same room,
this mewling wind (the hatching storm)
and beneath it the sea's voice, blown from the bight;

same stool, same square of sea-washed light
like the window's dazed dream-self spread
slightly skew at the foot of the bed;

many mis-shaped shadows and under the window,
in a dance of dust-motes, storm-wrecked Hero,
Hero dérangé

I stand
tip
toe
my left
hand
clenched
on an iron
bolt
the right
reaches
out
head
height
to throw
the shutters
against
the squall.

I stand . . . I reach . . . From high on the wall
a lamp pours out its ochre flame;
the door, like a jailbird, knocks in its frame,

lets loose a slithery shoal of gusts.
The little flame thrusts, convulses, thrusts,
tugs on its stem like a held balloon;

through the shutters, a glimpse of capsized moon,
very pale and windworn, blown on her back –
There is so much, Leander, that I lack.

I can't sit tight, as other girls do.
I cannot be a harbour for you.
The cold swims over my ankles, toes;

storm draws its breath. And so it goes.
All this in a blinkswhile – sunlight, floor,
a stuttering lamp, wind at the door.

I tense like a drum when the shutters slam,
and guide the slide-bolt home.

After Noon

At the turn of the day, as the hours unfurled
and the world came loose from the drift of the world,
I span while the seasounds flared and dwindled,

nerve-bound, fretful. The skittering spindle
had slipped three times from my hands when at last
I lifted the thumb latch, made for the path

and slid, half-crouched, where the hawthorn climbs,
barefoot, flushed, with blistering palms,
to stand in the bay and the bay's salt breeze.

I turned foursquare to your shore, my toes
in the crumbling surf that crept and shrank
at the sea's edge, and I could not think

or shape a thought except you would come.
Nothing around me spoke of a storm.
Nothing close at hand. Sand lay

in pools on the harbour wall; the sea
was empty, the sky empty of birds.
A few gulls stood where a skiff was moored.

There was black – there was *black* – but very far off
and barely a smudge – though still enough
to kindle an awful, in-blown wind

that tugged at my mind till it swayed and leaned
and sprang back straight like a birch tree shifting
in the wind's work of lowering and lifting:

twinge   *tremor*
over   *lower*
(Each gust the leaf-lapped mind blown barer.)

Water blinked, the sky was vast,
I could not rest. I wept. I paced
the violet shadowed sand and thought

to leave the signal lamps unlit
and settle the thing – you would not come.
What then? Oh what then? Time, the room

and night – the bed stretched out like a taunt,
like the gleaming skin of the Hellespont –
You say it would be a foolish thing

to chance the sea when the sea is wrong,
but you swam to me once before, with the bass
hum of a storm in your blood, when I kissed

the salt from your lips, your face, and held
my boy . . . By now the day had turned cold;
I looked out again at the crossing between

the shores that fringe your parish and mine,
so thin I could blot it out with a thumb –
which gave me strength of a kind. I grew calm

– almost at peace – and climbed to the house
to set the lamps in place.

GHOST

At the Farmer's Inn

Her lover lifts a Pilsner to his lips,
swallows it back
till the order arrives and they move like marionettes,
eat without talking.
Devilled kidneys, sea bass, crème brûlée.

The waitresses angle their hips between tables and carry
the plates in the air,
straight-limbed as matadors. Meanwhile, the men at the bar,
afloat on their barstools,
are baying like seals; a forest of backs occludes

both the girl and her tongue-tied lover. Out of the window,
behind his head,
night falls between the slats of the trestle tables,
over the scutch-grass
and the sheep, bunched in the corner of a field.

The hubbub thickens the air like moth-wings, it beats
at the sides of her skull.
Meal over, the day's a done deal – the dawn and the dusk,
the seed, the eggs
they harvested at noon with the consummate needle,

drawing them off like tiny, luminous pearls
from the sea of her body.
Now they drink to the dregs of their coffee, call for the bill,
link hands above
the petits fours while fifty miles from here

along the unfurled ribbon of the street,
the lamplit miles
of motorway, in a clinic, a darkened room,
like mushrooms, *very*
whitely, discreetly, the longed-for lives begin.

Phone

She leans her head against it, listening hard,
the way the Indians in the films of her childhood
would press an ear to the ground to listen for hooves.

She's hardly slept; a little pool of violet
trembles beneath both eyes as they look out to where
a jogger has paused by the gate. The phone begins –

Good news, it says, then something she struggles to catch
and *definite signs* . . . The clock ticks on the wall.
The jogger passes. *Seven's a very good number*,

the voice goes on, as if it were only referring
to the lucky number of folklore and romance –
seven brides for seven beaming brothers

instead of a fragile clutch of embryos,
their fine net veils lifting in the breeze.

Inventory for a Treatment Room

Her two bare feet, six blue, translucent
overshoes that crackle
across the floodlit floor
with people

in them, one of whom's her lover;
laughter, many hushed,
expectant silences;
a stool,

white plastic, where a nurse will sit, coo-
cooing like a mother
hen, a speculum;
no windows,

no sea-breeze, but an air that hatches
occasional, tentative jokes;
a lamp on a long, extend-
able limb;

one purple treatment chair, whose empty
purple arms reach out
for her.

The Enormous Chair

Some rooms remain with us –
like this one, filled
with light enough to bleach
uncharted miles
of desert sand; a room
so impossibly bright
that once she's inside it she
can't for a moment remember
how it is she got here
or why there are nurses
padding about like kindly,
soft-footed camels;
a room with at its centre
a single chair
of the sort you might see at the dentist's
or beautician's
(except that it's purple,
except it's the size of a house,
except instead of arm-rests
there are *leg-rests*)
in whose luxurious
vinyl-cushioned depths
she's invited now to recline,
legs akimbo.

Far off, someone's stroking her left hand
very softly. Someone is calling her *sweetheart*.

Constellation

A lamp the size and shape
of a flattened planet

traces a graceful arc
and comes to rest

in the constellation of her
parted thighs.

Egg

What finally emerges from the door
with the nameplate over the lintel, reading 'Egg'

isn't in fact a pale, ovoid creature
blinking into the light of the treatment room;

it's only the Polish embryologist,
petite and cheery in her gloves and scrub cap

and looking for all the world like one of the girls
serving on the bakery at Sainsbury's –

except instead of iced buns she is carrying
the world's two smallest humans, deftly clinging

to the edge of her pipette, the brink of being.

Inkling

Last night I sensed a taking root
under the bonecage of my heart,
a stirring, shifting; something not
quite of a breath or heartbeat's weight.

It was the inkling of a soul.
Now I shall have no peace at all
till he's caught and fastened, nested in
the cradle of my pelvic bone.

Then, in the coracle of my womb,
I'll carry him gently, every inch home
though the hour is late
in the lengthening light

to the crook of my arm, the bay's curved shore,
water-lapped, twilit, secure.

Leaves

First, one – smallish, yellow –
drops on the vertical, out in the hedge-dark lane.

> What she has learned: that in the earliest stages a woman has no way of telling if she is 'with child'. No blood tests, sticks, divining rods can guide her. The dogma she holds to, the very air she moves in, becomes waiting.

A second, a third,
headlong into the garden.

> Who was it who first drew attention to the body's presentient qualities? (She has seen it referred to as 'wisdom' but wisdom is going too far.) For instance, how the walls of the dough-soft womb will thicken, prove, to house an approaching egg. Soft landing, baby!

A wind blows up and larger leaves, tea-coloured,
pirouette on a south-east slant.

> What she knows: that a forming blastocyst has a shell, that the shell will dissolve till all that remains is the embryo – hatched, exposed and, like an astronaut, adrift.

The lawn is strewn with leaf-shapes,
turning and lifting.

> With luck (the more she waits the more she sees that luck has everything to do with it), the embryo will land on the wall of the womb – a boot on a dimply patch of moon – and sink itself in.

Hope spreads a creaky wing, full-span inside her,
and folds it again.

> See-saw margery, back and forth. Her mind is like a length of bladderwrack (as heavy and as damp) to

be lifted and dragged, hauled to the shoulder, several
times hourly, out of the sea of her thoughts.

Along the wall, leaf-clusters, bodies of leaves,
barely moving now in the shapeshift breeze.

What she most fears: that a thing picked up is not always held. A silvery sprat in the mouth of a heron, a latch-key dropped in the dark – not missed till you're pocket-plungy and empty-fist, moonlit at the door, the elbow-height gleam of the keyhole.

Stray leaves dip and dinnle in the gutter.

Ghost

She stands for a long time, next to the brightening window,
the quiet expanse of bed like a field behind her;
below her the lane, the bed-like field beyond.

The Kaffir lily's ablaze by the gate, the pigeons *cu-*
coo ru cu-coo. But she's mute as a nun
in her blue flannel gown; she levels her gaze on the sill –

the thick gloss paint, the silver nail file,
the shop-bought testing-stick she's prised apart,
in pieces now beside the weeping fig . . .

She takes it all in, like a small, controlled explosion:
here is the inch-long stiff, absorbent pad –
a stopped tongue, the damp on it still; and the plastic housing

with its cut-out windows. And here is the latex strip
(two lines for yes), the single band of purple
and beside it the silvery ghost of a second line

willed into being – frail as the arm of a sea-frond
trailed in the ocean – but failing to darken or turn
into more than a watermark.

Lapse

Put simply, the womb
was an open palm:
glabrous, dumb,
it had not known
to close. Just that.
Or else, like the fist
of an infant, it
fumbled, failed,
knowing to close but
not to remain
that way – how
long. Or when.

Pledge

Chiel, adrift
in the deeps of the future,
twiripe, yet-to-be
son or daughter,
if you had come
out of your dark to where I am
these are the things you'd have chanced upon:
sunlight and the changeful air
with its brood of noises – helicopter, dog-bark,
many song-filled, open-throated birds,
the knocks and echoes of neighbouring yards –
and the garden itself that all day long has been spawning
bee-hum and shadow, endlessly, bee-hum and shadow . . .

But you did not come
so I bide the while, calm,
like a fishing-net spreads itself, wide under water;
I give myself over, shell and shelter,
child, my own. By and by with the push of the wash
I'll usher you in.